EDGE
BOOKS™

AMAZING MILITARY
Robots

BY SEAN STEWART PRICE

CONSULTANT:
RAYMOND L. PUFFER, PHD
HISTORIAN, RET.
EDWARDS AIR FORCE BASE HISTORY OFFICE

CAPSTONE PRESS
a capstone imprint

Edge Books are published by Capstone Press,
1710 Roe Crest Drive, North Mankato, Minnesota 56003
www.capstonepub.com

Library of Congress Cataloging-in-Publication Data
Price, Sean.
Amazing military robots / by Sean Stewart Price.
p. cm.—(Edge books. Robots)
Audience: Grades 4 to 6.
Summary: "Describes various robots and robotic vehicles used by the U.S. military in
combat and reconnaissance work"—Provided by publisher.
Includes bibliographical references and index.
ISBN 978-1-4296-9917-4 (library binding)
ISBN 978-1-62065-776-8 (paperback)
ISBN 978-1-4765-1556-4 (ebook PDF)
1. Military robots—United States—Juvenile literature. 2. United States—Armed
Forces—Robots—Juvenile literature. 3. Robotics—Military applications—Juvenile
literature. I. Title.
UG450.P75 2013
623—dc23   2012033233

Editorial Credits
Aaron Sautter, editor; Ted Williams, designer; Eric Gohl, media researcher;
Laura Manthe, production specialist

Photo Credits
Alamy: AF Archive, 29; Courtesy of Boston Dynamics: 21, 24; DVIC: SSgt. J.R. Ruark,
15, U.S. Air Force/Master Sgt. Scott Reed, 17, U.S. Air Force/Tech. Sgt. Michele A.
Desrochers, 7, U.S. Navy/Mass Communication Specialist 3rd Class William Weinert,
22; Getty Images: Fox Photos, 14; Image provided courtesy of Army Research Lab
(ARL): 27; Newscom: EPA/Andy Rain, 18, WENN Photos/ZOB/CB2, 25, ZUMA
Press, 5; Public Domain: 9, 11; Wikipedia: Public Domain, 12, 13, U.S. Air Force/Lt
Col Leslie Pratt, cover

Design Elements
Shutterstock

Printed in the United States of America in Stevens Point, Wisconsin.
092013   007758R

Table of CONTENTS

The Three Ds

Imagine a war being fought in the far future. Rubble flies when an explosion blasts through a wall. A shiny metal figure with a huge gun then steps through the smoke. Nothing will stop this robotic warrior from completing its mission.

Robot soldiers were once found only in science fiction stories. But today military robots are being used on battlefields around the world. Robots can do many tasks once done by soldiers in war zones. Robots are often used for the "three Ds" of military life—jobs that are dull, dirty, or dangerous.

Some robots are used to do the heavy lifting on the battlefield. Soldiers often have to carry a lot of heavy equipment on their backs. But the Squad Mission Support System (SMSS) can haul about 1,200 pounds (544 kilograms) of equipment. This unmanned robotic transport vehicle can go over any kind of ground. It is driven by either remote control or voice commands.

 The Squad Mission Support System can carry the same amount of equipment as a squad of 10 soldiers.

Military forces sometimes use robots for heavy demolition work. The Armored Combat Engineer Robot (ACER) looks like a remote-controlled bulldozer. But it can do a lot more than push dirt. ACER can easily plow through dirt, chop down trees, tear through walls, or tow wrecked vehicles. It can even charge into a burning building and spray foam and water to put out fires.

Enemy fighters often hide in buildings unfamiliar to soldiers. In these cases, soldiers use a PackBot to safely explore a building and look for enemies. PackBots are about the size of a small suitcase and weigh about 40 pounds (18 kg). A soldier can simply throw one through a building's window and let it go to work. Its camera can help troops find any **booby traps** hidden inside the building.

booby trap—a hidden trap or explosive device

What makes a Robot?

All robots are machines. But not all machines are robots. Scientists disagree on how to define the word "robot." However, at least four things are needed for a machine to be considered a robot.

• Sensors: devices that measure changes in the outside world
• Processors: devices that study information from sensors and tell a robot how to respond to its surroundings
• Effectors: tools or instruments that allow the robot to perform actions
• Power source: a source of energy that allows a robot to move and do its job

Historic Robots of War

Machines have been used in wartime for hundreds of years. But World War I (1914–1918) marked the first time robotic machines were used in combat. Most robots at the time did not work well. But people learned from them to build better robots for future wars.

The Land Torpedo

The land torpedo was a small armored tractor that carried up to 1,000 pounds (454 kg) of explosives. The land torpedo was guided by a remote control attached to a long wire. It was supposed to roll into enemy trenches and then be triggered from a safe distance. However, the war ended before the land torpedo could be built in large numbers.

The Electric Dog

The Electric Dog was a small robotic cart used to help carry supplies on the battlefield. When a light beam hit a lens in the cart, it caused two batteries to switch on a small motor. The Electric Dog then moved slowly in a straight line to follow the light.

The Kettering Bug

The Kettering Bug was the world's first flying robot bomb. This small airplane had a 15-foot (4.6-meter) wingspan and carried a 180-pound (82-kg) bomb. The Bug flew a preset distance that was determined by the number of times its propeller spun around. Once that number was reached, the engine shut off and the Bug's wings fell away. The Bug then fell to the ground and exploded.

FL-7

German FL-7s were the only robots to see much action in World War I. These robotic motorboats carried 300-pound (136-kg) bombs. They were designed to ram into and destroy enemy ships. Each remote-controlled boat was connected to a wire that was several miles long. A boat's controller usually stood in a high tower or flew in an airplane to guide it. One of the most successful FL-7 attacks happened in October 1917. One FL-7 struck the British warship HMS *Erebus*, causing severe damage to the ship's hull.

The Kettering Bug was invented near the end of World War I. None were used in combat.

World War II

In 1898 American inventor Nikola Tesla discovered that machines could be controlled with radio signals. His wireless invention was widely ignored during World War I. But scientists later began using radio signals to control machines in World War II (1939–1945).

Operation Anvil was a U.S. Navy program to create flying bombs. The Navy took regular bomber planes and packed them with explosives. After takeoff, a nearby plane or ship would use radio signals to guide a plane to its target. However, the explosives used often blew up unexpectedly. None of the flying bombs did much damage to enemy targets.

Human pilots controlled flying bombs during takeoffs and then parachuted out.

124639

OR ★ V

Germany's Goliath bombs were like small tanks about the size of a wheelbarrow.

Germany's best robot weapon in World War II was an antitank bomb called Goliath. It carried up to 220 pounds (100 kg) of explosives. Soldiers used a remote control to steer a Goliath up to an enemy tank and set it off. Germany built 7,500 Goliaths during the war. But the robotic vehicles were slow. Opposing troops often cut their control wires before they could explode.

Shrinking Computers

After World War II little progress was made in military robots for several years. But soon advances in computers allowed scientists to create new kinds of robotic machines.

In the 1950s computers were as big as a large room. But in the 1960s scientists created new electronic devices such as **microprocessors**. These tiny devices made it possible to create much smaller computers. Smaller computers soon allowed scientists to create new kinds of robotic weapons and vehicles.

Vietnam War

During the Vietnam War (1959–1975) robotic vehicles were used mainly for airborne reconnaissance. The remote-controlled Model 147 Lightning Bug was an unmanned jet plane. It could fly up to 62,500 feet (19,000 m) high to take pictures of enemy positions. Lightning Bugs flew thousands of missions during the war.

 microprocessor—a computer processor contained in an electronic computer chip

reconnaissance—a mission to gather information about an enemy

A Robotic Victory

In Operation Desert Storm (1991), the U.S. Navy began using unmanned Pioneer aircraft to hunt for targets. A group of Iraqi soldiers saw one of these planes and began waving white sheets. The Iraqis knew the Navy was about to open fire on them and wanted to give up. It was the first time that human soldiers ever surrendered to a robot.

Today's Fighting Robots

In the late 1990s the U.S. military had only a handful of unmanned drone airplanes. But today U.S. forces use many kinds of robots. From unmanned aircraft to robotic weapon systems, these advanced machines are helping to keep U.S. soldiers out of harm's way.

Predators

Pilots fly remote-controlled Predator drones from thousands of miles away. Predators can stay in the air for as long as 24 hours. They carry cameras that can read a license plate up to 2 miles (3.2 km) away. They also use radar to see through smoke and haze.

drone—a remotely controlled aircraft

radar—a device that uses radio waves to track the location of objects

Reapers

Early Predator drones carried only cameras. They could observe enemy troops but not fire on them. U.S. soldiers soon began attaching bombs and missiles to Predators to attack enemy positions. Robot makers then decided to build armed drones such as the Reaper. These attack planes are larger and more powerful than Predators. They can carry 3,750 pounds (1,700 kg) of laser-guided bombs and missiles.

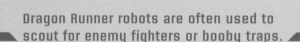

Dragon Runner robots are often used to scout for enemy fighters or booby traps.

ROBOT FACT

TALONs and Dragon Runners are famous for working under extreme conditions. One TALON robot got hit three times by machine gun fire and kept on moving.

TALONs

TALON robots are small robotic vehicles that can be picked up and moved by one person. TALONs carry several kinds of cameras, including night-vision and **infrared cameras**. TALON robots are often used to look for survivors in bombed-out buildings. Soldiers also use them to safely disarm roadside bombs from a distance. TALONs can be operated by remote control from more than 3,000 feet (914 m) away.

Dragon Runners

The Dragon Runner is small enough to fit inside a soldier's backpack. This rugged robot is tough enough to be dropped out of a moving vehicle. Dragon Runners are designed to be a soldier's eyes and ears in the field. Each robot is equipped with several cameras, microphones, and motion detectors.

 infrared camera—a camera that locates objects by heat

MAARS

The Modular Advanced Armed Robotic System (MAARS) is based on the TALON robot. But it can do a lot more than simply scout an area. It can be armed with a machine gun or grenade launcher and used in combat. MAARS can also be equipped to shoot pepper spray or smoke. An attached loudspeaker can also be used to demand enemies to surrender.

AlphaDog

AlphaDog is designed to haul supplies over long distances. It moves just like a large dog—but without a head. It's designed to walk across sand, snow, mud, and ice. If someone tries to push AlphaDog over, it regains its balance and keeps going. It can carry 400 pounds (181 kg) of supplies across 20 miles (32 km) within 24 hours.

ROBOT FACT

AlphaDog also acts as a portable power source. Soldiers can plug computers, cell phones, and other devices into its portals to recharge batteries.

The Phalanx Close-in Weapons System can fire up to 4,500 rounds of ammunition per minute.

REMUS

Remote Environmental Monitoring Units (REMUS) were originally built for mapping coastlines and reefs. These underwater vehicles often dive more than 300 feet (91 meters) deep. They work faster than human divers and aren't affected by darkness or cold water. During Operation Iraqi Freedom (2003–2011), REMUS robots used **sonar** and other sensors to find mines and explosives in waterways.

R2-D2

Artillery shells and missiles move too fast for people to shoot down. But the Phalanx Close-In Weapons System is able to track them and take them out. Soldiers began calling this high-tech system R2-D2 because it looks similar to the robot character in the *Star Wars* movies. R2-D2 is armed with two huge machine guns and is used to protect ships and Army bases from enemy attacks.

 sonar—a device that uses sound waves to find underwater objects

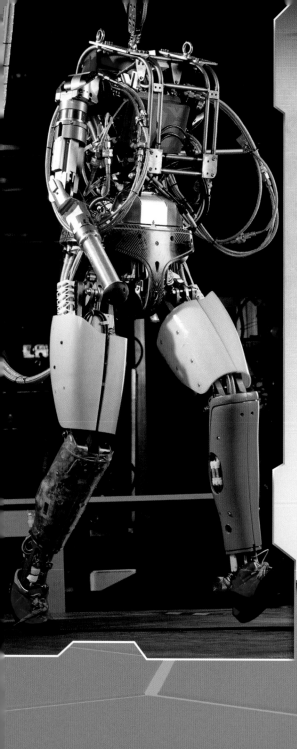

PETMAN

The Protection Ensemble Test Mannequin (PETMAN) is a **humanoid** robot that moves just like a person. It's built to act humanlike in many ways. PETMAN can even sweat like a person. The robot's main task is to test clothing designed to protect soldiers in chemical or biological attacks. There are no current plans to use PETMAN in combat. But it may help scientists learn to build a better robot soldier in the future.

ROBOT FACT

Some self-guided robots guard national borders, military bases, and nuclear waste sites.

BEAR is very strong, but it is gentle enough to carry soldiers without injuring them.

BEAR

The main job of the Battlefield Extraction-Assist Robot (BEAR) is to carry battle victims to safety. BEAR is strong enough to lift about 500 pounds (227 kg). BEAR's cameras and microphones allow its operator to know what it sees and hears. BEAR can also be used to carry supplies or hunt for booby traps.

 humanoid—shaped somewhat like a human

What Does the Future Hold?

Many of today's robots perform like land vehicles, planes, or people. But robots in the future could have incredible abilities. As technology advances, military robots will continue to evolve.

Oozing Into Battle

ChemBot was an experimental shape-shifting robot built in 2009. The white blob was designed to squeeze through tight spaces to spy on enemies. ChemBot was never used in the field and is no longer an active project. But scientists are working on new soft robots that may have future military uses.

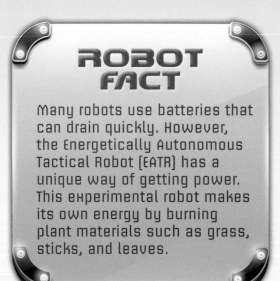

ROBOT FACT

Many robots use batteries that can drain quickly. However, the Energetically Autonomous Tactical Robot (EATR) has a unique way of getting power. This experimental robot makes its own energy by burning plant materials such as grass, sticks, and leaves.

Bugbots, such as this dragonfly robot, are designed to look and move like real insects.

FLies on the WaLL

Soldiers often need to learn what's going on in enemy locations. But going in is risky. In the future soldiers may send in a swarm of "bugbots" instead. Scientists are working on a robotic insect program called Micro-Autonomous Systems Technology, or MAST. These bugbots could be programmed for several different missions. Some could secretly spy on enemies. Others could look for dangerous materials or weapons. Still others could be used for search and rescue missions.

War Against the Machines?

Military robots can give armies a big advantage on the battlefield. Sometimes human soldiers can become hungry or tired and make mistakes. But robots are not affected by these conditions. They rarely make mistakes while following their programming.

However, robots can't tell friend from foe. What happens if a robot targets innocent people? Soldiers can judge different situations to make decisions. But robots don't have that ability.

How would someone fight robots that are simply following their programming? People might try to shoot at the robots. But a better option might be to hack into the robot's computer with a virus. In the future viruses could be used to shut down robot warriors or even cause them to self-destruct.

Most experts say robots can't disobey orders. But what could happen if a robot's programming began to **malfunction**? Would it begin attacking innocent people? Would anyone be able to stop it? These questions and more need to be explored as scientists create more advanced military robots of the future.

 malfunction—failure to work correctly

films like *The Terminator* explore what might happen
if future robot warriors turned against people.

29

Glossary

booby trap (BOO-bee TRAP)—a hidden trap or explosive device that is triggered when someone or something touches it

drone (DROHN)—a remotely controlled military machine; usually an aircraft

humanoid (HYOO-muh-noyd)—shaped somewhat like a human

infrared camera (in-fruh-RED KAM-ur-uh)—a camera that locates objects by heat

malfunction (mal-FUHNGK-shuhn)—failure to work correctly

microprocessor (my-kro-PROSS-ess-uhr)—a tiny computer processor contained in an electronic computer chip

radar (RAY-dar)—a device that uses radio waves to track distant objects

reconnaissance (ree-KAH-nuh-suhnss)—a mission to gather information about an enemy

sonar (SOH-nar)—a device that uses sound waves to find underwater objects; sonar stands for sound navigation and ranging

Read More

Alpert, Barbara. *U.S. Military Robots.* U.S. Military Technology. North Mankato, Minn.: Capstone Press, 2013.

Gifford, Clive. *Robots.* New York: Atheneum, 2008.

McCollum, Sean. *The Fascinating, Fantastic, Unusual History of Robots.* Unusual Histories. Mankato, Minn.: Capstone Press, 2012.

Internet Sites

FactHound offers a safe, fun way to find Internet sites related to this book. All of the sites on FactHound have been researched by our staff.

Here's all you do:

Visit *www.facthound.com*

Type in this code: 9781429699174

 Check out projects, games and lots more at **www.capstonekids.com**

Index